The Pink Experience

by Toya Richmond-Spencer

LET'S RETHINK THAT
Atlanta, GA
www.letsrethinkthat.com

Toya Richmond-Spencer
ministertoya@gmail.com
Facebook: Toya Richmond-Spencer

The Pink Experience
Copyright © 2015

Dedication

This book is dedicated to my three children, Tricie, Kailyn, and Malachi, and my ride or die, my mother. They are the reason I chose to fight so hard to live. This book is also dedicated to all the great women that have stood on the promises of God and fought and survived and also to those who have succumb to this dreaded disease and received their ultimate deliverance. I also want to dedicate this book to my beloved cousin, Terrence Partee.

Acknowledgments

First and foremost, I would like to thank my **Heavenly Father** for His grace and His mercy. I thank Him for getting me the courage and the ability to write this book. I know that without faith it is impossible to Him, for it is impossible to please Him, and He is rewarder of them that diligently seek Him (Hebrews 11:6). I cannot thank Him enough for deeming my life worth saving and transforming me into the person I am today. I want to thank my Lord and Savior Jesus Christ for affording me the opportunity to commune with my Heavenly Father. Without Jesus and the Holy Spirit, my survival story would not have been possible.

Special thanks to my mother, **Patricia Richmond,** for being my ride or die and being with me through each and every chemo session, every doctor visit, and just for being there through my battle. Thanks to my family for the sacrifice of love for taking care of me and my kids when I was not feeling my best. I must acknowledge my cousin, **Felicia Washington Baker**, for encouraging and uplifting me through my battle and for orchestrating my support person.

I also would like to thank my sister survivor diva friend, **Stephanie Turner Price**, for the laughs, the talks, the cries, the prayers, the encouragement, and the friendship. Thanks to my sister survivors **Krystal Henry** and **Vicki Dotson**. Krystal, even though we are miles apart, you made a very lasting impression on me. Thanks for the talks, the encouragement, the prayer, and just a listening ear. Vicki, we have been rocking since we met in the support group session. Thank you as well for being there. WE made it through together!!! To **Tonya and Craig Dickerson,** thanks so much for you all support and encouragement. Love you all to LIFE!!!

I want to thank **Bishop Kevin & Co-Pastor Linda Willis** and the **New Life In Christ Church** family for keeping me uplifted in prayer. To my spiritual mentor, **Evangelist LaTrice Ryan,** thank you for building me up and being an example of what a true Woman of God is supposed to be. Your selfless love, your kind heart, and your tireless effort to encourage women everywhere and especially on your team, is something that I am truly grateful to be a part of. I do not take it lightly or for granted the assignment of you being in my life.

Special, special thanks to my BIG BABY and my oldest daughter **Kiundria Antrice!** Thank you for helping me with your little siblings when I needed you. From picking them up from school to giving those baths and putting them in the bed, I really, really appreciated the selfless things that you did for me, my Love.

To **Derrick M. Tennial,** thank you, sir, for allowing me to tell my story and being my publisher and my editor and for sowing into my life. This project will not be possible without you. Thank you for seeing the writer in me when I could not see it myself. Thanks for the encouragement!!

To **Nicole Jackson,** after 30 years of friendship, you still believed in me and helped me when I needed you. Thanks friend!!

To **Rev. Cathy McKinney and the women of The Prayer Closet,** thank you for standing in the gap and praying for me when I could not pray for myself. Thank you, thank you, & and thank you! You all mean the world to me. Thank you for allowing me to strengthen my gift. Love you all much!!

And to all the ones that supported me through this trial in my life that I have not mentioned above, trust me, your kindness and thoughtfulness did not go unnoticed! I appreciate you all and to those that didn't support me, I appreciate you as well!!

Peace and Blessings,
Toya Richmond-Spencer

Introduction

    A rocky six-year marriage resulted in a divorce for me in 2012. I walked away with two more jewels, my daughter and son who are both special needs. I was already a single mother of one prior to the marriage.

    I was angry at everyone. I was angry at God about my marriage. "Why didn't God do something about my marriage?" as much as I prayed about it. I was angry with my ex-husband for leaving and forcing my hand in the divorce. I was angry at my parents for interfering in my marriage. It was more stressed than I could handle. The remnants of the divorce lingered as I looked at my two children living daily knowing he was not there to assist me with raising them as he is often times absent physically and all of the time financially.

So, there I was, divorced, three children, and what I thought was the ending of one journey was the beginning of another. I floated in and out of relationships to fill the void and to occupy my time. In May 2013, my cousin was diagnosed with colon Cancer and seven weeks later he succumbed to this dreaded disease. He was only 42. I remembered it like it was yesterday the day that he transitioned to life eternal. I saw his eyes and saw that the tears that would not stop flowing as if he knew that this life was over. The last thing he said was to clear the room because he wanted to get some rest. However, even after this, life kept moving, the world kept turning but, it seemed as if I were at a standstill.

November 5, 2013

God,

What are these pains in my breasts that I am feeling? They are not bothersome, but this is something that I have never felt before. Is it something that I should be worried about or should I just dismiss them because of my age? Well, I guess I am not that old to be experiencing just random aches and pains, huh? I am not going to claim anything. God, you told me that my words are powerful, and I shall have what I say. So, I am not speaking anything into existence, but I am going to ask my friend Tonya and my cousin, Sharon just to be on the safe side. They are both nurses. They should be able to tell me something.

November 10, 2013

God,

    What is this dream about? Did you send this to me? This dream can't be from you. This has got to be the work of the enemy. In the dream, I was in a doctor's office and the nurse told me that I had Cancer. I turned to her and asked what stage and she then told me that it was stage two. I woke up abruptly and rebuked the dream in the name of Jesus, calling forth healing and binding up any and every infirmity that was trying to come against my body. I have to admit. That dream scared me. It's only been a few months my cousin died of Cancer. Now I am having this dream. What does it all mean?

December 15, 2013

God,

    This pain that is occurring is something that I am not familiar with. I realize the dream that I had, but I believe that it wasn't from you but from the devil. The dream was too real...almost like I was experiencing an out of body experience. This dream could not possibly be from you, so I am going to keep rebuking the dream and cut the caffeine and sweets out of my diet like Tonya and Sharon suggested might be the source of this pain. I drink too much coffee and eat too many sweet anyway....

God,

      I've decided to begin the New Year with a new healthy lifestyle that consists of a diet and an exercise regimen. I really hope that this will make this pain go away. The pain is not consistent, but I do still feel it from time to time. So that makes me wonder that maybe, just maybe that this dream was just figment of my imagination. My church member Corey asked me and our other church member Kisha if he could be our personal trainer. Now Corey has a great physique - chiseled abs, nice forearms, but he is married, and I have to keep it strictly professional, but God... He is very athletic and seems to know what he is talking about concerning health and wellness. I'm not sure if he does this on a regular. Maybe he wants to use us as his guinea pigs or something. Anyhow, we decided to give him a try. My apartment complex has a workout facility and space to do circuit training. His price is affordable, and I really need to get rid of my "kangaroo pouch" and love handles. Geesh, my son is four years old, and I am still using him as an excuse for the weight gain. I can't use that excuse forever. Well, it's time to make a change and develop my body into what I would love to see when I look into the mirror. Besides what's the definition of insanity? It is doing the same thing over and over again, but expecting different results. And God, by no means, am I insane!!

January 21, 2014

God,

My exercising and weight loss is going well. Although there are times that I believe Corey is killing me, I can see a tremendous change in my body. My stomach is becoming flatter and my love handles are diminishing. I feel great, I have more energy, and I am sleeping better. The pain I was experiencing a couple of months ago is almost nonexistent. May be Tonya and Sharon were right. May be there's nothing to worry about. It was simply way too much caffeine and sugar in my diet. I've lost a whopping 15 pounds and I'm feeling pretty darn good about myself and I also am eating healthier even though I have my usual "cheat day" on

Sunday. I just can't miss Momma's Sunday dinner. Who can miss candied yams, cabbage, fried corn, baked or fried chicken, hot water cornbread, and homemade peach cobbler? I am getting hungry just thinking about it! I just try not to over indulge...lol! Even though I'm happy with my progress, I still need to go to the doctor though. Working this temporary job, I can't really afford to take off. I am not making much money and the more I take off, the less my check will be. I just can't afford to miss work and sit in a doctor's office at this time. So, for now, I'm just going to have to put the thought of making an appointment out of my mind. Whatever this pain is, I'm sure it's just a trick of the enemy and I am going to proclaim healing and walk in faith.

February 1, 2014

Lord!

Why won't you let me sleep? You know I have to get up in the morning to get the kids ready for school and get myself ready for work. I can't be late. Maybe if I just roll over and get into another position I can fall back to sleep, but it's no use, God. I can't sleep now, especially after what you just told me when you had me to get up and lay before you. As soon as I began to talk to you, that dream flashed before me. I saw the doctor office and the exam room. I was sitting alone and scared. Then, the unthinkable happen, I heard those words again "You have CANCER"!! I asked the doctor in the dream what stage I was in and he told me "STAGE 2." Oh no!!! Surely

God you didn't wake me up out of my sleep to bring this "nightmare" back to me. Please, God, please! I don't want to go through that! Please don't make me go through that!

But God, I can't ignore the other part you said to me, "It will be for your Glory." But Father, I don't want to go through that. The very thought of the "C" word frightens the living daylights out of me, but Father, you said to me, "It will be for my glory. How can you know me as a healer if I have never healed your body? This is a test of your faith and this sickness is not unto death." I am scared...I'm trembling. This can't be you. This has to be a trick of the enemy.

February 14, 2014

God,

      Today was my last day at work. What better way to celebrate Valentine's Day than to be unemployed and "un-booed"?!?!? On the flip side, I actually really enjoyed the people that I worked around though. This assignment was actually supposed to last only for two months. however, you turned that it into six months and on top of that, I got a raise. Thank you, Father!! (Praise Break). Since my temporary assignment is ending, it's the perfect time to go get checked out before my benefits expire. I'm ready to go ahead and put this "to bed" and to be sure that this dream that I had was not from you. I know we have had a conversation about it, but I just don't believe that was you! I don't want to be disobedient, doubtful, or rebellious and not do what you tell me to do. I am just trying to walk in faith and stand on your Word. I know that faith is not a denial of a thing or situation; however, it is still something that I do not want to face. Help me, Lord!

February 17, 2014

HAPPY BIRTHDAY TO ME!!! Still unemployed and "un-booed," but I am grateful that you allowed me to see another "Born-day." YAYYYY ME!!! I guess I will do the tradition of the family going out to dinner and them singing "happy birthday "off- key. Besides that, I guess I will get in here, and call the doctor and make that appointment to get checked.

February 17, 2014 @9:17 pm

I called the office and of course, the nurse asked me why I wanted an appointment and with whom did I prefer to see. I told her that I did not have a particular doctor that I wanted to see because I have been seen by them all even all the way to the nurse practitioner. I told her I was fine with the first available appointment. She scheduled me with Dr. Martin on Wednesday, February 19th at 10am. Excellent! The kids are in school and I do not have to worry about who will be watching them. The appointment is set, and I can finally get some answers even though the pain is still not consistent or even bothersome. It just appears from time to time, but I want to make sure that my health is not in jeopardy.

Today was my appointment. I had all kinds of butterflies in my belly. You know the nurse did the usual triage by getting my weight, blood pressure, temperature, and check my pulse. Then she asked me the dreaded question of "What's the reason for your visit today?" I told her that I had been experiencing dull shooting pains in my right breast. She made a note of it and took me to take into an exam room. She told me to undress "waist up" and to cover with the paper gown and the doctor will be in shortly. After about 20 or 30 minutes, Dr. Martin came into the room and asked me the same questions that the nurse had just asked. How annoying! So, again repeating myself for the third time, I told him that

I was experiencing dull shooting pains in my right breast. Dr. Martin immediately said that if I was experiencing pain, he was sure that it was nothing to be worried about. If it was something serious, it wouldn't hurt. Anyways, he examined my breast and asked me again to tell him where the pain that I am feeling is located. He started the breast exam again, stopped, and started again. By this time, I was thinking to myself that he is just trying to get a "FREE FEEL." After the examination, he said he didn't feel like there was anything to be alarmed about and the pains that I am having should subside because pain, again, is usually not associated with anything. And if it (the condition) is more serious, there will not be associated with pain. Cancer just simply does not hurt. I gave him this look as if I needed some further confirmation or documentation to assure me that everything is alright. Dr. Martin then said if it would ease my mind and reassure me, then he will write out orders for a diagnostic mammogram and ultrasound. I quickly said, "Yes it will." He had the nurse to schedule my appointment.

February 28, 2014

I have an appointment at for a diagnostic mammogram and ultrasound. My mom is going with me for moral support and also to treat to breakfast afterwards at Cracker Barrel. Oh, how I love their breakfast!!! Just the thought gets me hungry. Mmmmmmm Hmmmmm!!!!!

Anyway, I am going early so I can finish early. Don't want to keep Cracker Barrel waiting!!! LOL!

February 28th @ 10:49 pm

God,

    I went into my appointment this morning thinking the procedure would have taken an hour... no more than two, but FOUR HOURS LATER, I was still there... The tech took so many pictures of my right breast from every angle possible. After the ultrasound, I went back to take another picture with the mammogram machine. By this time, I had gotten a little paranoid and impatient. All the other patients had come and gone and now it was lunch time...and I was still there...You know what that meant? No Cracker Barrel breakfast for me.

    The radiologist called me into the office. All kind of thoughts were running thru my head.... Is this the procedure? Did everyone else have to talk to the doctor? Is that why I am here so long? When I sat down in the chair in front of her desk, I noticed that she had two pictures laid out in front of me - one of my left breast and one of my right breast. The radiologist introduced herself and asked me how I was doing. She then asked me did I see a difference in the pictures. And of course, I said "yes." There was a big white mass that appeared to be in my right breast. Then she said it! In her expert opinion, she believed it was Cancer. She said she was 99% sure that it was...Cancer. At that time, I could feel blood rushing to my head and I felt faint and I literally blanked out. What? This can't be! My eyes swelled, tears begin to roll, and my chest began to hurt. I couldn't hardly breathe. The radiologist was still talking, but I couldn't hear her. All I could hear was the sound of Charlie Brown's teacher...I know she said plenty more. I do remember her saying she didn't know why I had come into the office, but it had to be you, GOD, bringing me in there because I would have never found this mass until it was too late." She told me the mass was in the lower quadrant of my breast. Even though she gave me her expert opinion, she said wanted to be 100% positive and the only way of doing that was to schedule a biopsy. She scheduled the biopsy for March 5th.

I'm not sure what to think. I am so numb. It is still kind of surreal for me. I know you revealed it to me in the dream, but I was always taught that a dream like that had to be from the enemy and to never accept it. I am still not willing to accept it. I will just use the "Out of sight, out of mind" method and try not to dwell on this issue. All you ask of me, God, is to have faith the size of a mustard seed and I can command this mountain to move and it shall be done and that NOTHING shall be impossible for me (Matthew 17:20). So, this mountain needs to move out of my way. God, you told me that it will be for your glory, so I know you are going to astonish the doctors by performing a miracle on Wednesday. I just know that when the doctors try to perform the biopsy, they are going to find nothing - NOT-A-THING!!! That is what you have to mean by the situation being for your glory. I am going to fast and pray and present my body as a living sacrifice and you will hear my prayer and grant me my petition. I will decree and declare, and it will be done. A miracle will be performed. I have peace about the situation and now I can sleep and not be worried.

God,

My biopsy is scheduled for today. So, I'm fasting and praying and laying before you. You are going to astonish the doctors and not allow the mass to be present. God, you did tell me to speak it, decree it, and declare it, and it shall be established, didn't you? Didn't you say in your Word that I can speak to the mountain to be removed and it shall be done? Didn't you say in Isaiah 55:1 that your Word will not return unto you void, but it shall accomplish what it has set out to do? God, I know that you showed me in a dream that whatever this is will be for your glory. A miracle will be performed. So, I am standing on your promises. No, I am not accepting the enemy's report, but I believe the report of the Lord. I am going to keep speaking healing and continue to ask other believers to be in agreement with me as well.

March 5, 2014 @ 7:31 am

Lord,

    I am on my way to my biopsy appointment with my ride or die by my side - my mom. My mom asked me how I am feeling. I told her I was fine. I'm trying not to worry her even more seeing that my dad that is having cataract surgery today as well. I really didn't know how to respond or explain to her that I was standing on your Word and still proclaiming that you have the last say so. I am walking in with my head held high and I have the confidence that you will not let me down. Again, Faith is what?!? The substance of things HOPED FOR and the EVIDENCE of things not seen (Hebrews 11:1). So, I have great expectation that a miracle will be performed today!!! So, LET'S GO!!!

March 5, 2014 @ 9:36 pm

Lord,

I am fighting with myself, the enemy, and with you. I am fighting with myself because of fear; the enemy wants me to lose faith, and with you for showing me the dream and asking you to perform a miracle how I saw fit....

Before the biopsy, the radiologist, Dr. Hunt, that performed the procedure entered into the room and he told me he was 99% sure that it is Cancer by just looking at mammogram and lab results. I quickly told him, "God has the last say so." He gently agreed, but firmly stated again that he was sure it was indeed Cancer, but we are hoping for positive results. I laid on that cold, hard table ready for this machine with this HUGE needle on the end to enter into my body. They inserted the numbing medicine. All I heard was the needle attached to this machine sounding like a drill that is going in and out of my breast. My emotions were running crazy. God, what happened? Did you hear my request? Why didn't you grant my petition? It's ok. Maybe you are saving the news for the end. They are gonna test whatever it is that they find in my breast and it will not be Cancer. It's going to be a cyst or something to that nature. I am fine. This is only a test. Dr. Hunt stated that the test results will take two days. This will be a longest two days of my life. However, I am believing you for a positive result. It will be in my favor... and then you will be glorified.

March 7, 2014

God,

     I received a call today that changed my life completely. At 10:30 am, Dr. Hunt called me with a definitive diagnosis. He called with a very upbeat attitude, yet the news was not very gratifying. He told me the pathologist's report confirmed that it is Cancer. The dream was real! The conversation with You was real. Here I am... an otherwise healthy 39-year-old female that just lost 15 pounds, and I've been diagnosed with Breast Cancer. Sitting there on the phone with him, my life flashed before my eyes. My body went numb. Lord, how could You allow this to happen to me? This doesn't even run in my family. You know I have two little ones to raise and one that is getting ready to graduate from high school. I can't leave them. Lord, I can't handle this?! First, my husband walks out on me and turns his back on his family. Now I'm unemployed, no income, a family member just succumbed to Cancer, and now the doctor tells me that I have this!!! I feel like I am tied up in a knot. I can't talk, I can't move, I can't believe it. Oh my God! Really?!?! I did all of this fasting, praying, speaking the Word, and I still didn't get the results that I was looking for. What am I going to do?

March 7, 2014 @ 10:32 pm

God,

So, after hearing my diagnosis and having a pity party, I shared it with my mother, my children, my ex-husband, and my closest relatives. I knew my youngest two will not understand what mommy has to go through, so I did not feel a need to share that information with them. My mother and my daughter were devastated, and I had to be strong for them and reassure them that I will be alright and that you will heal me. When I mentioned it to my ex-husband, he took it hard as well because his mother passed away at the age of 48 due to complications from chemotherapy treatment. However, when I told my cousin, Felicia, she immediately told me that "I know that you will be alright" and kept repeating that I was going to be alright. That really blessed and uplifted me. I am still not sure if I wanted too many people to know. There is a part of me that wants to be isolated from the world and the other part of me wants the whole world to know. I am going through so many raw emotions: grief, fear, denial, anger, frustration…. Then I can't help but think about Terrance, my cousin, who just died of Cancer. I know just because he died doesn't mean I am going to die, but I got to put my big girl panties on. I will not allow the enemy to win.

March 8, 2014

God,

    Your Word is filled with scriptures on healing and you stated that all I need is Faith the size of my mustard seed and I can move mountains (Matthew 17:20). So, I decided to put your Word on every mirror, wall, bedroom door, kitchen cabinet, and in the living room. I have to be constantly reminded of your Word. The enemy will not win during this battle. What the enemy means for bad, I know you will turn it around for my good.

My cousin, Felicia, is really trying to help by getting me a support team together. I am not so sure if I want to talk to anybody as of yet. I am still trying to wrap my mind around this whole "Cancer" thing and to be bombarded by questions of "how I am feeling" or "do you have any questions" or even "is there anything I can do to help" is something that I am not sure I want to hear right now. The way I am feeling, at this moment, my answers might be "Yea, there is something you can do; Get rid of this cancerous tumor growing inside of me" or "Just leave me alone because I just do not feel like being bothered." Not trying to offend anyone, but that is just how I am feeling.

God,

    Since my diagnosis, I have been going round and round in circles with my primary care doctor about getting scheduled for a surgeon and about an oncologist about what? First, he didn't really want to send me to get a mammogram, but after finding out that the pain I was feeling was actually Cancer, he wanted me to come back to see him first before he sent me for treatments. He probably wanted to go crawl under a rock and was hoping that I was not gonna sue him for malpractice. However, he did send me. Lord, his nurse was so unprofessional and so disrespectful that I had to drive back to the doctor's office and speak to the owner of the practice in order to receive proper referrals to an oncologist and a surgeon. While waiting for the surgery, I am still believing you to perform a miracle on my behalf. Isn't that what your Word states?!? That miracles, signs, and wonders shall follow them that believe? And I know that your Word will not return unto you void, but it shall accomplish what it has set out to do. So, allow this tumor to disappear when I go for surgery. Father, let the doctors be astonished. Do it FOR ME LORD!!! In your son Jesus' name, AMEN!!!

March 14, 2014

Dear God,

What are you trying to do to me? The storms just keep on coming. First, divorce, next death of a relative, then unemployed, followed by breast Cancer, and then my son getting diagnosed with Autism and my daughter with Developmental Coordination Disorder. Not really sure about what all of that means for them. I am really going to do my research and figure it out. Whew!!! God, you said that you would not put more on me than I can bear, but this seems a tad bit much. Why? I really don't understand why? Let alone, why me, Lord?!?! I was a good wife, mother, and faithful to you. This is so HARD!!! It is almost unbearable. I'm not sure what to do or how to do it, or who I need to do it with!!! God, you have people in this world that are not experiencing what I am. They are living the LIFE with no worries or cares. They are prospering and not even concerned with doing your PERFECT will. I am not even sure they are concerned about doing your permissive will. I gave up the "party" life, accepted your calling on my life, yet I am facing all of these trials and tribulations. Don't your Word say that you have never seen the righteous forsaken or his seed begging for bread (Psalms 37:25). It sure feels like I have been forsaken...

March 15, 2014

I did a little research on Autism and Development Coordination Disorder. I found out that autism is a neurodevelopmental disorder. People with it have impaired social interaction, meaning they do not pick up on social ques like the rest of us. They also may have difficulty communicating and become frustrated like when they can't get out what they can't express themselves. They also might be limited in their behavior and repeat certain behaviors over and over again. Many people with autism never live independently. My son may never be able to live independently. Then my daughter, Lord, she has is also neurological disorder than can cause her to have difficulty in controlling her speech, reading, writing, and spelling. It may also cause her to have difficulty in math as well as understanding instructions. Oh, God...I knew something was not quite right, but all of this? I am so overwhelmed. Lord, I thought you would not put more on me than I can bear. My diagnosis, my daughter diagnosis, AND my son diagnosis...all in a few weeks? How can I really do this? How can I really be patient enough for them? Right now, I am believing - NOT hoping for the best. Lord, if you CAN HEAL me, I know you can heal them too...

March 27, 2014 @ 6am

God,

    Today is the day. The day I get my healing. My prayer is still that you are going to astonish the doctors when I go for them to put this wire in my breast. Let there be NO TUMOR in sight!!! Standing on your Word....Standing on your promises. Like.... Speaking those things that be not as though they were. Since I was made in the image of you and my words are powerful just like yours, I believe I can call those things into existence. I know that Faith is not a denial of things, however, DO IT LORD!! Get rid of this tumor! I am getting ready to walk into this office and I believe that the tumor is gone.

March 27, 2014   @ 12 noon

God,

I walked into the room with the mammography machine; all kinds of feelings are coming over me... feelings of anxiousness, fear, curiosity, and nervousness. Hoping and wishing that my prayers were answered. Lord, I know you said that this is just a test of my faith and that you will heal me SO THAT I can be a testimony of your healing power. Ok, God! I will endure the process because it is truly looking like what I am asking is NOT going to come to pass. The tumor showed up, the radiologist had to put this wire through my breast, and then the surgeon removed the cancerous tumor growing in my breast. God, this is not how this day was supposed to go...

March 27, 2014 @ 6pm

God,

   Why am I still in this hospital? I thought this was supposed to be an outpatient procedure. Lord, I feel terrible. I am so dizzy, nauseated, and in pain. I can't keep anything down, so they are keeping me hydrated with fluids from an IV. I never thought that I would be hurting like this. All of this, a lumpectomy, for a 2.5 cm tumor?!?! This is ridiculous. I was told that was supposed to be a 45 minute to hour procedure took over 2 hours? Jesus! Even though I am stuck here, I heard the best news ever. The surgeon said that he got the entire tumor out. However, he still needs to see if the Cancer traveled to the lymph node that was closest to the site. It will be three or four days before he will not find that out for certain. What a relief!!! Thank you for this wonderful news. I know that you have the last say so and I know that you have already told me that I am healed, but Lord, please don't let it spread to the lymph nodes. If it has gone to the lymph nodes, it could have spread throughout my body and set up any or everywhere. You are the Great Physician and my Healer. I'm trusting you, Lord...

God,

    I woke up with an attitude of gratitude today. Just thanking you for getting that tumor out. I'm still very nauseated and in a lot of pain. Thank you, Lord, for this pain pump!!! This is good stuff. Now I see how Michael Jackson became addicted. But Lord, my breast! I was a double DD cup and now the majority of my breast is gone. That seems a bit extreme for just a 2.5 cm tumor!! That's not very big. Why is this incision so big and why is most of my breast gone? It's almost like I have had a mastectomy. Was the surgeon confused and thought I was to have a mastectomy instead of a lumpectomy? Is that why the surgery took longer than expected? Is that why I had to stay in the hospital? God, you got to help me with this one.

April 3, 2014 @ 10am

God,

Today, I had my follow up visit with surgeon. It's been a week since my surgery and I am still full of questions and anxiety. He checked my incision, pulled the drain out of the incision sight, and gave me the pathologist's report concerning my lymph nodes. I am healing very well. I questioned him about the amount of tissue that was removed, why my breast looks this way, and why my incision is so long. He explained that the amount of tissue he had to take out was approximately 6 cm to get a "good feel" and a "good margin" of the tumor. There was some benign tissue as well as cancerous tissue. The pathologist's report stated that the Cancer has NOT traveled to the nodes. HALLELUJAH!!!

Thank you for revealing to me that the Cancer was in my body and to go get checked. I still question why so much of my tissue is gone even though I am elated that it had not metastasized to other parts of my body. If I had not yielded to your voice, Lord, it could have been much, much worse. I know it took me awhile. Who wants to believe they have Cancer? I didn't then...and it's hard to believe now.

God,

  I had an appointment for a follow up visit with my oncologist. She went over the pathologist's report from the biopsy and from the day of my surgery. The two pathologist reports were different, so she decided to order another test called UNC-D, which will determine which results are correct. Still, more than likely I will have to have 8 rounds of chemotherapy. It's a light dose, so the chemo shouldn't take my hair out or cause nausea. That was not what I wanted to hear, but I will take it. After the chemotherapy and radiation, I will have to take a daily hormone therapy pill called Tamoxifen for the next five years!!! This pill will cause my body go into menopause. I will experience all the symptoms of a woman that is going thru menopause   Menopause...at 39? Lord, help! It's not like I wanted to have any more kids, but I'm not sure if I am ready for what all comes with it hot flashes, mood swings (which I have enough of), headaches, hair loss, increase chance of heart attack, and so on and so forth.

But God, when she checked my incision sight, she immediately jumped back and asked "Why does your breast look the way that it does? A lumpectomy was not supposed to look like that way. She labeled it as "severe" in my chart and referred me to a plastic surgeon for breast reconstruction. Wow, God, I am thankful. Call me vain, but I don't want to live my life deformed.

God,

    I just got a call from my Cancer doctor with some very disappointing news. Much to her surprise, the UNC-D test were read different from the other two pathologist's reports. I am in the slight positive range of progesterone that the Cancer I had possess, which means that the Cancer is somewhat attractive to the hormones in my body. However even though it is a low number, she's going to treat me as if I have Triple Negative Breast Cancer. The only way to fight Triple Negative Breast Cancer is to administer a stronger regimen of chemotherapy, which may cause hair loss, nausea, vomiting, and fatigue...all the things I didn't want to happen! What?!?!? I told her that I am doing the first treatment we talked about — the light dose of chemo and radiation for 8 weeks, and I will go on faith and hope that that treatment will do what it is supposed to do. My doctor, of course, was against my decision but agreed stating if that's what I want then that's what we will do. I slammed the phone down and I broke down in tears. Yet another curve ball thrown at me. I have already received two different diagnoses and now here is another one. God, I thought you said that this will be for your glory. Why are you putting me through this?! I don't know how much more of this I can take...

God,

How can I know that you are a healer or a restorer if I do not allow you to heal or restore? I heard you say, "Praise the Lord, my soul; all my inmost being, praise his holy name. Praise the Lord, my soul, and forget not all his benefits - who forgives all your sins and heals all your diseases and heals all your diseases (Psalms 103:1-3) and to write down all the questions I desire to ask the doctor and to call her. I did, but she was unavailable to come to the phone. God, I really had to weigh out the importance of keeping my hair or saving my life. I believe my greatest fear is how will I look without any hair? Will I look funny? Will I get stares? Will I look sick and feeble? How am I going to deal with the constant questions? How are my children going to take? Will I look weird to them? Is keeping my hair more important than being here for my children? Is keeping my hair more important than living a life more abundantly according to your Word? Is keeping my hair more important than putting my family thru unnecessary grief because I want to be stubborn? I believe your Word and I am willing to stand on your promises that I walk in divine healing. Whatever comes my way, I know you will be with me and protect and strengthen me. My doctor finally returned my phone call at the end of her day. She answered all my questions. I humbly apologized and told her that I will do what she recommends. Thank you, Lord, for reminding me of who I am and who's I am.

April 20, 2014

God,

     This journey has already been full of disappointments, triumphs, heartache, loneliness, frustrations, tribulations, headaches, and anxiety. I have only been dealing with this for a couple of months and I haven't even started the "chemo" treatments yet. I am finding out people that say that they are there for you aren't really there for you. The ones that you thought would be your biggest support will turn their backs on you. They will stab you in the back and stomp on your heart in order to protect themselves even though you are going through this rough patch in your life. People just don't care. I understand now what your Word says in Psalms 18 that we should put no trust or confidence in man or woman and that it is better to take refuge in you. People are so FICKLE!!! There is no sense of loyalty or integrity nor self-worth or compassion to either your fellow man or woman. Many days I sit, and my phone doesn't ring. No one calls to see if I'm okay or if I need help, especially financially since I'm not working. No one has offered to even to bake me a cake or bring me a fruit basket. I have three kids, two of which have special needs which are definitely very difficult to handle at times. They have so much energy. They will not sit down. They are running through the house falling and putting things in their mouths. So, I have to pay extra attention to them. God, please place it on someone's heart to volunteer to be godparents and take them off my hands sometimes. Even though I was in the hospital for three days, I sure did enjoy the fact that I could rest fully and not be bothered.

April 24, 2014 @ 1 pm

God,

Today was my first treatment of chemotherapy. It went well. No side effects except I am a little fatigued, but my emotions are all over the place: fear, worry, doubt, and self-pity is consuming me. My biggest cheerleader and supporter, which was my Mother, sat with me thru a grueling four-hour treatment. My appointment was at 1:00, but I didn't leave to almost 5:30. The people at the clinic are great, very compassionate, and supportive. They made me feel comfortable and I received all kinds of goodies, snacks, and moral support. Even with all of that, I still wished I had that someone that my heart longed for. The person that I wished was there didn't really deserve my heart. He stepped on it...twice, but my mom is always there no matter what. I just feel like I am always relying on her for everything even when I was married. I feel more of a burden than a grown, independent woman that has three kids.

God,

   Just one day after my first chemo treatment, I had the pleasure of seeing my daughter going to her senior prom. I was so overwhelmed with joy and happiness that I almost forgot I just had chemo. I was so excited, but yet I was a little sad as well. My daughter has finally reached the age of maturity and she is no longer my little girl. I just hope and pray that I was a great example of what a mom should be. In some ways, I think that I am not. I don't think that I taught her what it means to truly value herself. Boys... men will come and go in and out of her life, but she needs to know her self-worth. Tricie tells me all the time that she will make me very proud. She really does not realize that she already has. She's an honor roll student, she works, she helps with her younger sister & brother, she keeps the house clean (even if she tries to fuss at me), she does my hair when needed, and she has not gotten pregnant unlike some of her friends. Whew!! I give all the praises to you!! Thank you, God, I am so elated that I have a daughter like this. I just ask that you bless her with her heart's every desire. Her father, her grandparents, and her uncles were there, one which drove from Nashville to witness this momentous occasion. And thank you for allowing me to see this.

OMG!!! The symptoms from the chemo treatments have kicked in. It was like someone hit me in my head with a bat. My head was hurting so bad that not even my pain meds helped it and then my body was aching soooo bad. I felt like I had the flu or something. I didn't want to eat, drink, or anything. All I wanted to do was sleep. I had chills, diarrhea, and nausea. Lord, please let this cup pass me by. In the midst of what I am going through, I have something to be really to be grateful for. My little brother was in an accident while returning home to Nashville. Even though the car was totaled, and he had to rent a car to get him back home, I THANK YOU for sparing his life! It could have been much, much worse. Father, you told me that the prayers of the righteous do avail much. I am so glad I keep him covered under the blood of Jesus. Thank you, Jesus, for being the pilot and keeping his guardian angels encamped around him.

April 30, 2014 @ 10:16 am

God,

    I need to talk. I have so many random thoughts coming in and out of my mind that I need to release. You did tell me to cast all of my cares upon you for you care for me. So, you wanted them, here they are! At this point in my life, I feel that I really dont know which way to turn or which way to go. I feel kind of lost. I know I am going through this for a reason, but I'm not sure what it is or why I was chosen. I know I'm not the only one that has experienced this, but it feels that way. Everyone has their own personal struggles or tests or tribulations that they have to deal with, but some seem to never face adversity. I know that I am only on the outside looking in, but I feel like I have accomplished nothing but heartache and bad decisions in my life that have crippled me. At this time, I have no income coming in to fall back on and I am really trying to dig in deep to find that hidden talent that will thrust me into my purpose and destiny. What is it, Lord? What do I need to do? What are you trying to teach me? I feel lonely, confused, crippled, stagnated, sorry, etc. Sooooo many emotions are running through me. I know that I have the power to trample on serpents and that no weapon that formed against me shall prosper. It may be formed, but it shall not flourish. I know trials come just to make me stronger. Well, Lord, if you send anything else my way, I just don't think that I can bare it. Father, send your peace and comfort right now... In Jesus' name!

May 8, 2014

God,

     Now you know that I have been praying for you not to allow my hair to fall out. How about today the very thing I am praying against starts to happen. My hair has started to shed. Now, Lord, I thought we had an agreement. That as long as I asked in your son's Jesus name and believe it that it shall come to pass. So, I guess that was just my heart's desires and not your will, huh?!? Well, can you stop the shedding and just let's be satisfied with what has already happened? You know I have heard of many reports that some women did not experience hair loss. Can I be in that number? I don't need the stares nor the constant questions. I'm not really sure how I would look with all of my hair gone. Lord, I know it's just hair and it can grow back, but what do I do in the meantime? I have seen women wearing those wigs. Some of those wigs look cheap and classless, especially the free ones. What if the wig falls off while I am at church? Please Lord, spare my hair!

May 11, 2014

  It's Mother's Day!! I am spending it up in Murfreesboro with my daughter trying to get her on the cheer squad for college. You know that she is very good at that type of stuff. We are really praying for her to make the squad, and hopefully she will qualify to get a scholarship. However, do you know what else is bothering me? Yep, you guessed it! My HAIR!!! It is shedding so bad that I had to go buy a cap from Walmart to cover my head. Lord, you know I was still standing on Faith that this will not happen.

May 11, 2014 @2pm

Lord,

My daughter did not make the cheer team. My hair continues to fall out! UGH!!! Can you say a double whammy?!?!?! This is a very hard pill to swallow. It is very hard looking at clumps of hair coming out and not only that, my head was terribly itchy and sore. What's that about, Lord? You told me that I am worrying about the wrong thing and that you are trying to do something through me? That you are doing a new thing in me and that you will make a way for me in the wilderness (Isaiah 43:19). I hear you, Lord. This is just so hard for me to handle, but I do know that I can do all things through Christ which strengths me. Lord, please just give me the strength...

May 13, 2014

Lord,

My heart is heavy, and I cannot stop crying!! Father, why did you pick me to go through this!! I know you said that you would not put more on me than I can bear, but this is crazy!!! I left my job at Walmart thinking I had a better opportunity with another job, only to end up fired and disrespected because I would not date the owner. You called my cousin home just 7 weeks after he found out that he had colon Cancer. Next, I started working a temporary job only for the assignment to end and then to find out that I have Breast Cancer!! Oh, not to mention that my husband walked out on the kids and I to move back to his hometown. LORD, LORD, LORD!!!

I know that trials are just a test of your faith and the race is not given to the swift nor to the strong, but to the one that endures to the end (Ecclesiastes 9:11). Are you listening Lord? Can you hear me? I'm crying through my tears. I am crying through my pain! Can you feel my pain and anguish? Speak Lord....I need to hear your voice. Can you please say something? Maybe I am talking too much...maybe I am complaining too much. I am going to get into a place of silence, so I can hear you speak to my heart. I hear you Lord....I heard you say not to fear or be dismayed for you are my God and you will strengthen me, help me, and uphold me (Isaiah 41:10). Physically, I do not like what I am going thru. However, I know spiritually that I can do the impossible.

May 15, 2014

God,

I am still a little down trotted; however, a good friend of mine came over to cut the rest of my hair off. I still cannot fathom to look at myself in the mirror. I cannot even phantom what I look like without hair. I am so ashamed that I cannot go to the barber shop for him to cut it. Today, my oldest daughter is graduating from high school. This should be one of the most exciting times in my life, but instead I am facing hair loss and self-esteem issues. Luckily, I did prepare in the case something like this happened. I was taught by my Bishop that "preparation time is never wasted time." And that definitely came in handy at this moment because if I had not prepared myself for the particular situation, I am not sure what I would do.

I keep a scarf or cap on my head at all times. However, while I was getting dressed for my daughter's graduation, I decided to finally take a glimpse of myself. I actually did not look half bad. In my opinion, I resembled the model Amber Rose which I considered an honor because I think she is a very beautiful woman, but I still felt ashamed and did not want the stares or the interrogations. Let me get myself together and focus on my daughter and her moment. I need to allow thanksgiving to consume me because if it had not been for you Lord, being on my side, there no telling where I will be. I want to thank you, Daddy, for allowing me to witness my daughter's graduation. Thank you for giving me peace that surpasses all understanding (Philippians 4:7), keeping me sane, and cleansing me from the inside out.

May 16, 2014

God,

It is time for yet another chemo treatment. Since my oncologist decided not to insert a Porta Cath, I have to get stuck somewhere in my arm or hand. This is okay if you have someone that knows how to find a vein and is not constantly sticking you erroneously. Needlessly to say, I did experience this, and she had to stick me in the back of my hand which is very painful, and she still didn't get it right. Where did she get her license and training from? She needs to go back to the basics because this AIN'T working! I need the supervisor or somebody on here that knows what they are doing. GEESH!!! Anyways, they finally got the IV in and the chemo started. During this treatment, I experienced burning and irritation at the IV site. The nurses had to apply a warm compress on the site during treatment. God, I have so much to do between today and tomorrow. Please do not allow any symptoms to surface and cause me to slow down. My daughter's graduation dinner is tomorrow, and I also have been asked to speak on a panel for my Breast Cancer support group concerning my diagnosis. I got to keep moving. Thank you for allowing me to have the strength to drive to and from my appointment. Thank you that I have hope in YOU and YOU will renew my strength. I will soar on wings like eagles; I will run and not grow weary, I will walk and not be faint (Isaiah 40:31).

May 17, 2014 @ 9:41 am

God,

   Today, I am participating on a panel concerning Triple Negative Breast Cancer and I also have to prepare a graduation dinner later on for my daughter. I am so grateful that I have been requested to participate with this group of women. It is indeed a pleasure and I give all Glory to YOU this morning. Father, give me the wisdom to answer all questions effectively and efficiently. Please hide me behind the cross and do not allow any flesh to glory in your presence. I know that it's only because of you that I live, breathe, and have my being.

God,

    The founder of the support group complimented me on my speaking ability and said she is going to have to make me something in the group like their minister, evangelist, or something. Wow!! God!! I am honored!! After the panel, I headed home to prepare for the celebration for my daughter. Along with the help of my parents & my BFF, the celebration was a huge success. It almost appeared as if we are experienced caterers or something. However, I am experienced some swelling in my legs and feet, but no nausea or pain. Even though I am worn out, it is all worth it for my 1st born

Thank you for standing at my side and giving me strength, so that through me the message might be fully proclaimed, and all the people might hear it. And that I was delivered from the lion's mouth (2 Timothy 4:7).

May 28, 2014
_____

    Today, Father, we are on the road taking my daughter to get registered for orientation at MISU. My BFF, her godmother, paid for the trip and for all of us to attend the orientation. My BFF can be a difficult person to get along with at times because she is just as spoiled and stubborn as I am. However, she does have a heart for her god-daughter. Glory to God!!! Even though I am being tried in the fire, God, you are really providing for me and my children. My daughter got the chance to attend her senior prom; her dad paid for it all including her senior dues. I thank you Father for touching his heart at this particular time. Even though, there are many more bills I need to be paid, things

_____

my children and I need, our basic needs are being met. Hopefully, my unemployment claim will be approved very soon and that will help out tremendously. I really hate being at the mercy of others, but I am thankful that they are there to help at this time. This experience has really humbled me. God, show me the things that I should be concentrating on. I am not satisfied with the way I have lived my life thus far and I ask that you do what you need to do in and thru me. Transform me, conform me, restore my soul, create in me a clean heart, and renew the right spirit within me (Psalms 51:10). In spite of what I am going through, you are still my God and I am your child. You are sustaining me, healing me, and providing for me.

June 6, 2014

God,

It is time for my third chemo treatment. The last cycle went incredible well. Other than the rash and a little nausea, my side effects were very limited. Hopefully, I will have the same kind of cycle this time. God, please allow Ms. Ruby to be at the clinic to stick me. I don't want anyone else to do it. The last person could not get it right for nothing in the world. I looked on YouTube to learn how to do a head wrap. I think I did pretty well since I don't have any hair to fill it out. I guess a t-shirt will have to fill in for the lack of hair. Today, I am a little tired and drained. So, I am going to sleep through my treatment today. I hope my momma have her tablet to keep her entertained because I just cannot do it today. I am grateful and thankful that she is here to keep me company.

June 7, 2014

God,

    I got a wonderful surprise today from you. My unemployment has been approved and I received that financial blessing in the mail. I praise you God!!!! Now I cannot be so worried with financial burdens. At least something is coming in. I guess that's one less thing to worry about.

June 13, 2014

Dear God,

Today is absolutely horrible day. I'm already not feeling good from this chemo treatment. My head feels like I got hit in the head with a baseball bat. No amount of pain meds is helping. I sent my kids over to their grandparents, so I can have peace and quiet to rest. My stomach is upset, and I am nauseated. I feel weak and exhausted. However, while experiencing all of these uncomfortable symptoms, I receive a frantic phone call from my oldest daughter informing me about one of our relative (a 43 yr old woman) is calling her phone and cussing her out. I never in my life would I think I would experience that from her. Well, I actually cannot put anything pass her. But this was neither the time nor place to deal with such foolishness. I knew she was off her rocker but never to this extent. I'm not sure y I didn't think that she would ever stoop this low against me, but how foolish I was to think that. All of this happened because my daughter wanted to charge another $10 to do her and her daughter's hair. Crazy right?!? Mind u, she had been doing their hair and not charging them but $20 and staying up late even on school nights. U know the enemy always like to show his head when you are close to your breakthrough. Now, not only did that demon have the nerve to call my daughter with that foolishness but it was bad enough to call MY phone and tell me that she was going to do something to my daughter. Father, I know you said its okay to be angry but not to sin, but I am going to have to really repent for this one. How dare you call my phone and tell me that my daughter will not make it to college because you are going to shoot her. God, if that was a test...I definitely failed that one. I called her everything but a child of God. At that time, I had all kind of obscene words flying out my mouth. Who calls someone and threatens their child? The enemy that's who...didn't recognize him at first, but I did later. I acted all out of character. And the most upsetting thing I heard from her mouth was that she hopes I never goes into remission. So, she is wishing death on me? Is she hoping that you don't heal me? What manner of evil is that? Oh no, I got sooooo angry that I could see myself choking the life out of her.

I had to get this off of me... so, God, remove the anger that I have inside me. I cannot effectively go to the next level in you harboring this type of anger.

Dear God,

Today was my last chemotherapy treatment. YAYYYYY!!!! I made it!!! Praise God!!! This was one of the best days of my life. The best feeling was ringing that VICTORY BELL when I finished Chemo and they gave me a certificate and everything. At the end of my treatment, my oncologist wanted to see me and set me up for the last stage of my treatment which is radiation. She was excited about how fast I got through my chemo and how well I was doing. She began to tell me that my radiation will began in four weeks and will last for 6 weeks Monday thru Friday but would not last more than 30 mins. She examined me and told me if I had any problems that persisted after chemo please come in and let her know. But I will see her every 3 months. I asked her when will I get my scan that would let me know if I'm Cancer free? She then told me that I was Cancer free after surgery and that things we were doing were just preventive measures. HALLELUJAH!!! Even though I knew in my heart and my soul...it's was indeed good to hear those words come out of the doctor's mouth... That I'm CANCER FREE!! "Millions didn't make it, but I was ONE OF THE ONES WHO DID!!!" Praise God!!!!

June 28, 2014 @ 2am

Dear God:

Here I go again.... I'm up and cannot sleep. God, the last time you woke me up in the middle of the night, it was not good news that you were trying to convey to me. However, this night was much different. You began to speak blessings and favor over me. God, you told me that now is the time that you shall put your Word in my mouth and I shall speak what needs to be spoken. That you are NOW pouring out YOUR FAVOR and YOUR GLORY upon me and bringing forth in the gift that is inside me. Is there more God? I also heard you say that you are opening doors for me... opportunities, divine connections, people are just going to want to bless me and my vision. Double anointing, double favor, and double of Your Glory. I heard you also say, that you had to get me in the right place and purge out the things that was not like you. That this period was my transformation. I shall feel His power and His Fire from this day forth. I am setting your feet on a plateau. Eyes have not seen nor ears have heard what I about to do for you. You are my called and my chosen, my daughter. You will bless my name at all times and my PRAISE WILL FOREVER BE IN YOUR MOUTH. FOR I AM THE LORD THAT HEALETH THEE... I AM THE GREAT I AM... I AM WHO I SAY THAT I AM. FOR NOW YOU KNOW...The song "Great God" by Deitrick Haddon was playing in my head when I was awakening. The time is drawing near for my return and people are ignorant to the truth. Your family shall be saved and WILL support your ministry. Your children shall be blessed because of your obedience and your prayers. God you also stated that you are gonna open up my ears and eyes and you will start speaking to me ever so clear. The indigestion that I am feeling is not regular indigestion...it's you imparting your FIRE on the inside of me. HALLELUJAH!!!!

"When Jesus heard that, he said, This sickness is not unto death, but for the glory of God, that the Son of God might be glorified thereby."

John 11:4

Conclusion

I want to encourage those that have recently been diagnosis with Breast Cancer or even going through the "fight" of Breast Cancer. There are many emotions that you will feel, but do not allow that to question your faith. The Cancer is your condition and not your position. Remember the power that God has placed on the inside of you and not to give that power or authority over to the enemy. For the Bible says, we wrestle not against flesh and blood but against principalities, against powers, against the rulers of darkness of the world, against spiritual wickedness in high places (Ephesians 6:12). The enemy wants you to give up or give in and for you to relinquish your mind, body, and soul to him. Don't allow him to steal your health, kill your ambition, and destroy your faith. I declare that you are full of power, strength, and determination. I decree and declare that you are more than conquerors through Him who loved you (Romans 8:37). Believe the unthinkable, speak the unimaginable, Decree and declare the unbelievable because all God wants you to have is the faith the size of a mustard seed. Your faith will move mountains. Trust in the Lord with all your heart and lean not into your own understanding, in all your ways, acknowledge Him and He will direct your paths (Proverbs 3:5). You are capable of far more than you know.

Also, during this fight, I need you to build up positive emotion. Negativity, doubt, worry, fear, holding   onto grudges, frustration, harboring unforgiveness, etc. can allow sickness and disease to take place in our bodies. John 16:33 states that in this world you will have trouble but take heart, I have overcome the world. That simply means that trouble will come, trials will come, sickness will come, but be encourage and choose to be joyful in and through your storm because Jesus has already overcome that. Proverbs 17:22 states that a cheerful heart is good medicine, but a crushed spirit dries up the bones. I chose to laugh throughout my journey. So I admonish you to choose to have that same joy and happiness. God is not a respecter of persons. If He delivered and healed me, He will do the same thing for you. Command your health to be release back into you. Continue to fight for your health, your peace, your mind, and your strength. You are an OVERCOMER!! You shall have the VICTORY!!! As my mentor always say and you can say it too. MY NAME IS BREAKTHROUGH!!! So, whose report will you believe?

Five Stages of Grief

According to psychiatrist and near-death studies pioneer, Dr. Elisabeth Kübler-Ross, there are five stages of grief.

1. Denial
2. Anger
3. Bargaining
4. Depression
5. Acceptance

Whether you have been diagnosed with Cancer or experienced life-changing trauma or drama, you perhaps are experiencing or have gone through these stages.

Denial:

The first stage in the grief process is Denial, which is used as a defense against grief. In dealing with your current situation, you may have made statements such as:

- ☐ "I can't have Cancer"
- ☐ "I don't have Cancer."
- ☐ "The doctors have made a mistake!"
- ☐ "This changes nothing!"

Are you in denial about your Cancer diagnosis or prognosis or your current life situation?

_____

_____

_____

_____

Anger

Feelings of angry, resentful, and sometimes even hate may be directed toward God or anyone you blame for your current life situation. You may have made statements such as:

- ""What did I do wrong?!"
- "God, why did you let this happen to me?"

Who do you blame and/or are angry with for your current life situation?

_____

_____

_____

_____

_____

_____

Bargaining

In this stage, you may have tried to cut a deal with God to deliver you from your current life situation. You may have made statements such as:

☐ "God, please take this away from me. I will do anything."

☐ "I am believing God to deliver me."

Do you want to be healed or delivered from your current life situation because the reality of it is too overwhelming? If so, why? Are you still in negotiations with God for your healing and/or deliverance?

_____

_____

_____

_____

Depression

In this stage, you start to face reality and the grief actually sets in classic grief symptoms such as crying spells and isolation are exhibited. You may have made statements such as:

- "My life is over. I can't go on."
- "I have nothing left to lose - my family, friends, and God."

What part of your current life situation has caused you to be discouraged, despondent, and/or depressed?

_____

_____

_____

_____

_____

_____

_____

_____

_____

_____

_____

_____

_____

_____

_____

_____

_____

_____

Acceptance

You have finally come to terms you're your diagnosis or current life situation regardless of how that reality looks. You may have made statements such as:

☐ "I have Cancer."

☐ "This is my reality and I own it."

After reviewing the five stages of grief, honestly and realistically where are you? Have you accepted it?

_____

_____

_____

_____

_____

_____

_____

Healing Scriptures

Like David, there are times when we must encourage ourselves. What better way to do it than with the Word of God? During my Pink Experience, I posted these scriptures all over my bathroom mirror, my bedroom, and in other parts of the house to serve as a constant reminder of that God is a healer and that all I was going through would be for God's glory.

Exodus 15:26

> And said, If thou wilt diligently hearken to the voice of the Lord thy God, and wilt do that which is right in his sight, and wilt give ear to his commandments, and keep all his statutes, I will put none of these diseases upon thee, which I have

brought upon the Egyptians: for I am the Lord that healeth thee.

Psalms 103:2-3

2   Bless the Lord, O my soul, and forget not all his benefits:

3   Who forgiveth all thine iniquities; who healeth all thy diseases;

Psalms 107:20

He sent his word, and healed them, and delivered them from their destructions.

Psalms 118:17

I shall not die, but live, and declare the works of the Lord.

Proverbs 17:22

A merry heart doeth good like a medicine: but a broken spirit drieth the bones.

Isaiah 41:10

Fear thou not; for I am with thee: be not dismayed; for I am thy God: I will strengthen thee; yea, I will help thee; yea, I will uphold thee with the right hand of my righteousness.

Isaiah 40:31

But they that wait upon the Lord shall renew their strength; they shall mount up with wings as eagles; they shall run, and not be weary; and they shall walk, and not faint.

Isaiah 53:4

4   Surely he hath borne our griefs, and carried our sorrows: yet we did esteem him stricken, smitten of God, and afflicted.

Isaiah 53:5

But he was wounded for our transgressions, he was bruised for our iniquities: the chastisement of our peace was upon him; and with his stripes we are healed.

Jeremiah 17:14

Heal me, O Lord, and I shall be healed; save me, and I shall be saved: for thou art my praise.

Matthew 8:17

That it might be fulfilled which was spoken by Esaias the prophet, saying, Himself took our infirmities, and bare our sicknesses.

Mark 8:33-34

33 But when he had turned about and looked on his disciples, he rebuked Peter, saying, Get thee behind me, Satan: for thou savourest not the things that be of God, but the things that be of men.

34 And when he had called the people unto him with his disciples also, he said unto them, Whosoever will come after me, let him deny himself, and take up his cross, and follow me.

Mark 8:35-38

35 For whosoever will save his life shall lose it; but whosoever shall lose his life for my sake and the gospel's, the same shall save it.

36 For what shall it profit a man, if he shall gain the whole world, and lose his own soul?

37 Or what shall a man give in exchange for his soul?

38 Whosoever therefore shall be ashamed of me and of my words in this adulterous and sinful generation; of him also shall the Son of man be ashamed, when he cometh in the glory of his Father with the holy angels.

Mark 11:24

Therefore, I say unto you, What things soever ye desire, when ye pray, believe that ye receive them, and ye shall have them.

Luke 4:40

Now when the sun was setting, all they that had any sick with divers diseases brought them unto him; and he laid his hands on every one of them, and healed them.

Romans 8:2

For the law of the Spirit of life in Christ Jesus hath made me free from the law of sin and death.

Romans 8:11

But if the Spirit of him that raised up Jesus from the dead dwell in you, he that raised up Christ from the dead shall also quicken your mortal bodies by his Spirit that dwelleth in you.

2Corinthnians 10:4-5

4   For the weapons of our warfare are not carnal, but mighty through God to the pulling down of strong holds;

5   Casting down imaginations, and every high thing that exalteth itself against the knowledge of God, and bringing into captivity every thought to the obedience of Christ;

James 5:14

14   Is any sick among you? let him call for the elders of the church; and let them pray over him, anointing him with oil in the name of the Lord:

James 5:15-16

15   And the prayer of faith shall save
the sick, and the Lord shall raise him up; and if he have committed sins, they shall be forgiven him.
16   Confess your faults one to another, and pray one for another, that ye may be healed. The effectual fervent prayer of a righteous man availeth much.

1 Peter 2:24

Who his own self bare our sins in his own body on the tree, that we, being dead to sins, should live unto righteousness: by whose stripes ye were healed.

3 John 2

Beloved, I wish above all things that thou mayest prosper and be in health, even as thy soul prospereth.

www.ingramcontent.com/pod-product-compliance
Lightning Source LLC
Chambersburg PA
CBHW071945100426
42736CB00042B/2060

* 9 7 8 0 6 9 2 5 4 0 3 6 7 *